The Sunflower Family

The Sunflower Family

by Cherie Winner

photographs by Sherry Shahan

A Carolrhoda Nature Watch Book

 Carolrhoda Books, Inc. / Minneapolis

The author thanks the following for their time, patience, humor, and enthusiasm: Walter Fertig, Wyoming Natural Diversity Database; B. E. Nelson, Rocky Mountain Herbarium; Dr. Daniel J. Crawford, Department of Plant Biology, Ohio State University; and especially Dr. Ronald L. Hartman, curator of the Rocky Mountain Herbarium, Department of Botany, University of Wyoming.

This book is available in two editions:
Library binding by Carolrhoda Books, Inc.
Soft cover by First Avenue Editions
c/o The Lerner Group
241 First Avenue North, Minneapolis, MN 55401

LIBRARY OF CONGRESS CATALOGING-IN-PUBLICATION DATA

Winner, Cherie.
    The sunflower family / by Cherie Winner ; photographs by Sherry Shahan.
        p.   cm.
    "A Carolrhoda nature watch book."
    Includes index.
    Summary: Describes the physical characteristics of the composite family of plants, how they reproduce, their distribution, and various uses for some of them.
        ISBN 1-57505-007-2 (lib. bdg.)
        ISBN 1-57505-029-3 (pbk.)
        1. Sunflowers—Juvenile literature. 2. Compositae—Juvenile literature. [1. Composites (Plants). 2. Sunflowers.] I. Shahan, Sherry, ill. II. Title.
QK495.C74W56 1996
583'.55—dc20   95-46110

Manufactured in the United States of America
1 2 3 4 5 6 – JR – 01 00 99 98 97 96

For Peggy Werkmeister, my cousin and dear friend   —C. W.

For Dale: Macro mentor par excellence
                                        —S. S.

CONTENTS

As you walk outside in late summer, you see dandelions poking up through cracks in the sidewalk. Daisies and marigolds bloom in your neighbor's yard. In a field nearby, thistles and goldenrods nod in the sun, and a majestic sunflower towers over them all.

All of these plants are composites, members of the Compositae (kum-PAH-zi-tee) family. The Compositae family is also called the "sunflower family," because sunflowers are its most familiar members. The sunflower family is very large. It includes about 25,000 species, or types, of plants. Only 18 are actually sunflowers. Other composites such as daisies and asters resemble sunflowers. Still others, such as thistles, dandelions, and lettuce, look very different. Some composites are delicate plants just an inch high, some are shrubs, and some are trees over 65 feet (20 m) tall.

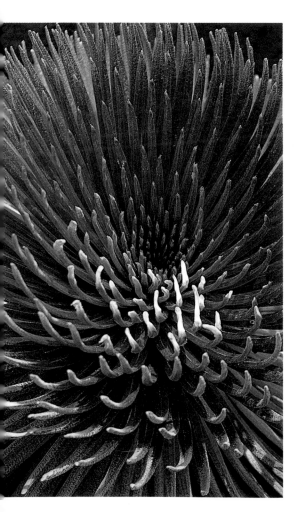

The blooms of many composites look like stars. This feature led to another name for the Compositae family: Asteraceae, from the Greek words meaning "starlike."

Composites first appeared in the mountains of South America over 30 million years ago. From there, they spread to every continent except Antarctica. They have **adapted,** or adjusted, to almost every kind of **habitat** on earth, from high mountains to tropical rain forests, from swamps to deserts.

Composites have also adapted well to humans and have moved with human travelers all over the world. Humans, in turn, have found many ways to use composites—as medicines, poisons, fuel, and food.

COMPOSITE FLOWERS

The one feature that all the different composites have in common is that what looks like a single flower is really a cluster, or **head,** of many tiny flowers. (The word *composite* means "made up of many parts.") The common sunflower *(Helianthus annuus)* is a good example of this. Each flower in the sunflower head is called a **floret** (FLOR-et). The florets in the center of the head are small and usually dark brown. Each of them has five equal-size petals that are joined together to form a tube. Thousands of these florets are packed tightly into a large circle called the **disk.** These small florets are called disk florets.

Larger florets around the outside of the disk are usually bright yellow or orange. These are called ray florets. Like a disk floret, each ray floret has five petals that form a tube, but in ray florets, one side of the tube is much longer than the other. Together, the disk and ray florets make the sunflower head look like a single large flower.

The common sunflower (Helianthus annuus)

A sunflower plant starts as a sunflower seed like the ones you may have fed to birds or munched on as a snack. When the seed is surrounded by moist, warm soil, it sprouts. Its growth is powered by nutrients stored inside the seed. A small stem with two leaves appears above ground. Over the next few weeks, the plant grows taller and develops more leaves. Chemicals in the leaves use sunlight to make food for the plant. Eventually it forms one or more heads.

At first, a sunflower head is a tight, hard bud. Surrounding each bud are leaflike structures called **bracts**. The bracts overlap each other to form a strong layer called the **involucre** (in-voh-LOO-ker). When the plant is ready, the bud opens to reveal the florets inside. The involucre holds the florets together and protects them from plant-eating insects.

The gazania (top left) *and the Mexican hat* (Ratibida columnaris, top right) *are both composites despite differences in the shapes of their heads.*

Many composites have heads that look a lot like sunflowers, but the heads of other species look very different. A sunflower head is nearly flat. Heads of other composites may be cup shaped or may bulge out in the center. The colors of the blooms may be very different as well. Ray florets may be pink, white, blue, purple, or dark red. Disk florets may be black, gold, or red.

The number of florets can vary too. Sunflowers have more than 2,000 disk florets and hundreds of ray florets. Other composites have no rays, like the Laramie false sagebrush *(Sphaeromeria simplex),* or no disk florets, like the large-flowered skeleton plant *(Lygodesmia grandiflora).*

Despite these differences, a close look shows that all members of the sunflower family have a composite head rather than separate, single flowers.

Above left: *Laramie false sagebrush* (Sphaeromeria simplex)
Above right: *The large-flowered skeleton plant* (Lygodesmia grandiflora)

10

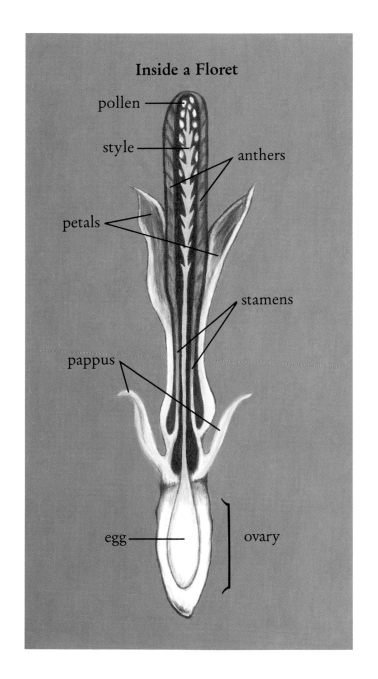

Inside a Floret

pollen

style

anthers

petals

stamens

pappus

egg

ovary

MAKING SEEDS

For any flowering plant, the function of its flowers is to produce seeds. To do this, a flower has some parts that make the seeds, some parts that protect the seeds, and other parts that help **disperse,** or spread, the seeds.

To produce a seed, a male reproductive cell, called a sperm, must join with a female reproductive cell, or egg. In most composite plants, each floret contains the parts that produce eggs and sperm.

In the center of the floret is a tall female structure called the **style.** At its base is the **ovary** (OH-vuh-ree), a chamber holding one egg. Five long, slender **stamens** (STAY-mens), which are the male structures, surround the style. The base of each stamen is attached to the petals. Each stamen has a puffy tip called an **anther,** which holds grains of **pollen** (PAH-lun). Each pollen grain contains two sperm. In composites, the five anthers join to form a ring around the style.

11

The outer disk florets of the sunflower mature sooner than the inner ones. Can you match florets in this photo to the stages of growth below?

At first, the petals of a floret are tightly closed (diagram 1). Then the floret opens (diagram 2) and the anthers poke up (diagram 3). Finally, the style grows up from inside the tube of anthers, carrying pollen with it. When the style is fully grown, its tip splits into two stigmas (diagram 4).

1   2   3   4

As the flower grows, the style pokes up through the ring of anthers, taking with it hundreds of pollen grains. When the style is fully grown, its tip splits lengthwise into two small arms called **stigmas.** The stigmas curl backward to expose their inner surfaces, which are very sticky.

At this point in a floret's life, insects play an important role. Beetles, flies, bees, and butterflies are attracted to the bright colors of composite heads. They come to the head to drink **nectar,** which is a sweet liquid held in small pockets just above the ovary in each floret. As the insect probes for nectar, it brushes against the style and anthers. Pollen sticks to the insect's legs and is carried off when the insect leaves. When the insect visits another plant, some of the pollen gets brushed off. If the second plant is the same species as the first plant, one or more of its florets is **pollinated.** Since many florets are clustered together in a head, an insect can pollinate many of them in one visit. In a few species, such as ragweed *(Ambrosia),* wind—not an insect—carries the pollen from plant to plant.

If no pollen is deposited on the sticky stigmas, the two arms curl back until they come into contact with pollen grains left on the lower part of the style (diagram 1). *Once the egg has been fertilized, the floret wilts* (diagram 2) *and the seed in the ovary begins to grow* (diagram 3).

1   2   3

When a pollen grain settles on one of the stigmas, a tube grows out of the pollen grain and down through the style to the ovary. The two sperm inside the pollen grain then travel down this tube and **fertilize,** or join with, the egg. Together the egg and the sperm make a seed. Because the pollen was from a different sunflower plant, scientists say that **cross-fertilization** has occurred.

If no cross-fertilization occurs, some species of plants can still make a seed.

The stigmas keep bending back farther and farther. Eventually they curl back so far that they touch the lower part of the style and any pollen grains the insects did not carry off. The process in which an egg is fertilized by sperm from the same plant is called **self-fertilization.** Cross-fertilization is usually better for the species than self-fertilization, because it produces offspring that are better able to survive disease and other stressful conditions.

After fertilization occurs, the petals of the floret wither and fall off. The ovary remains attached to the head and develops into a hard shell to protect the seed inside it. The entire structure, seed plus shell, is called an **achene** (ah-KEEN).

The achenes may drop out of the head as soon as they form, or they may stay attached to the head for a while. Eventually they all end up on the ground. Not every seed will develop into a new plant. A dry seed can survive in its shell for many years, but in order to sprout and grow, it needs to land in a spot with the right amount of moisture, sun, and good soil.

The pappus of this thistle achene is made up of many hairlike strands.

SEED DISPERSAL

Composites have developed many special ways of getting their seeds to places where they will have a good chance to grow. Some species, including the common sunflower, survive by keeping their achenes near the parent plant. When fully developed, the achenes simply drop to the ground.

Many species of composites rely on special features of their achenes to disperse their seeds farther from the parent plant. One such feature is the **pappus** (PAP-us), a ring of hairs, bristles, or scales on the top of some kinds of achenes.

Achenes of the common sunflower are larger and heavier than many achenes, and they have no pappus. This means that wind can't carry them very far, so they simply drop to the ground near the parent plant.

Left: *Dozens of long, downy pappi (the word for more than one pappus) make up this thistle head.*

In thistles *(Cirsium)*, the pappus bristles grow to about four times the length of the achene. Each bristle is covered with tiny hairs. The pappus acts like a sail, allowing even a light breeze to carry the achene a long distance—in some cases, even hundreds of miles.

The pappus bristles of the cornflower *(Centaurea cyanus)* help the achene move even after it has fallen to the ground. In dry weather, hooks on the bristles spring suddenly outward, making the achene hop along the ground. In wet weather, the hooks soak up water and fold back toward the achene. If the spot stays damp, the seed will sprout. If the spot dries up again, the hooks spring out again, and the achene takes another hop.

Above: *Achenes of the cornflower* (Centaurea cyanus) *have a complex method of dispersal.*
Below: *If you blew on this fuzzy dandelion head* (Taraxacum officinale), *hundreds of achenes would be sent off to sprout new plants.*

18

Right: *Burs of the burdock*
(Arctium minus)
Below: *The common cocklebur*
(Xanthium strumarium)

Some achenes, called **burs,** sport little spikes and hooks. These spikes may cover the whole achene, or lie in several rows along the shell. A bur sticks to whatever touches it—especially the fur of passing animals or the clothing of people walking by. Those animals and people may carry the bur a long way from the parent plant. When the achene is eventually brushed off or falls off on its own, the spikes help anchor the achene in soil, where the seed can sprout and grow.

In burdock *(Arctium),* the whole head forms a bur. The involucre on the back of the head develops prickly spines and curls up to form the outside of the bur. The mature achenes are on the inside. After the bur is carried to a new place, the seeds sprout to form a new clump of burdock plants.

19

In a few species, each plant actually forms more than one kind of head and uses more than one method of seed dispersal. *Gymnarrhena micrantha,* a small plant that is common in the Negev Desert in Israel, produces one kind of head near the top of the plant, about 1.25 inches (3.2 cm) above ground, and another kind just below the surface of the soil. Achenes from the upper heads are small and have a long pappus with many fine hairs. The wind easily blows them to new sites. Achenes from the lower heads are larger, heavier, and lack a pappus. These achenes usually don't disperse at all. They stay right there and start growing in the same spot their parent plant did.

Leaving some seeds near the parent and letting others disperse helps the species survive. The spot where the parent grew is obviously a good place for it. But if something harmful happens to that site, such as a flood, disease, or disruption by humans, the dispersed seeds will still have a chance to grow. Even if the original site continues to be a good place to grow, having some seeds disperse helps the species expand the area where it grows.

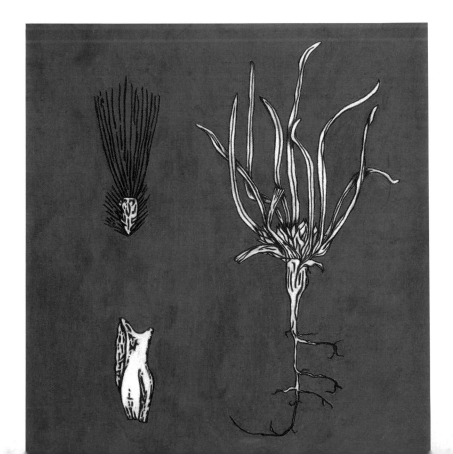

In Gymnarrhena micrantha, *the plant* (right) *produces two types of achenes* (left).

Composites are often found in flower gardens. The person who planted this garden helped aid dispersal by buying and planting calendula, *the orange flower in the foreground.*

Although composites can be very resourceful about dispersing their seeds, humans also lend a hand. The most obvious way we do this is by taking plants and seeds to other places where we think they might grow. But plants and people have also worked together to disperse seeds in ways no one could have predicted.

Rolling in the dust is a good way for a bison (right) to get hooked achenes stuck in its coat. The prairie sunflower (Helianthus petiolaris, below) used to live only along bison trails. Now it grows along roads and railroad tracks throughout much of the U.S.

Until the 1800s, the prairie sunflower *(Helianthus petiolaris)* lived only on the high plains of what is now Kansas and eastern Colorado. Its hooked achenes stuck to the fur of bison, who dispersed them all along the routes where they traveled and grazed. Then came dirt roads for horses and wagons, and eventually, railroads. The prairie sunflower's achenes hitched a ride off the high plains and took root farther and farther eastward. Staying close to roads and railroad tracks, they reached the east coast of the United States about 150 years after they started their migration. Today, prairie sunflowers grow throughout the midwestern and eastern U.S.

Smith's groundsel (Senecio smithii)

One of the longest known plant journeys was made by Smith's groundsel *(Senecio smithii)*. It originally grew at the southern end of South America. Two hundred years ago, whale-hunting ships sailing in the area accidentally carried some of the groundsel seeds to the Orkney and Shetland Islands, which lie off the northern coast of Scotland. The cold damp climate, rocky soil, and nearness to the ocean resemble its original home 10,000 miles (16,000 km) away. Smith's groundsel took root and now thrives there.

Opposite page: *Sagebrush* (Artemisia, foreground) *thrives in hot, dry places.*
Above: *Some species sport a single taproot* (left) *rather than a system of thinner roots* (right) *to help them survive dry periods.*

HABITATS

Composites can be found in almost every habitat on earth. But most composites have developed special features that allow them to grow and reproduce best in just one habitat.

More composite species live in desert or semidesert areas than in any other habitat. Some desert species live along streams or rivers. Others live far from water and have special features to help them cope with their dry environment. Their leaves may be tough and leathery or covered with tiny hairs, all of which help the plants hold water inside their leaves. Some species have shallow roots that spread over a wide area to soak up as much rainwater as possible. Other species have one long root, called a **taproot,** which can reach water deep underground.

Senecio aquaticus grows best in a marshy habitat, but not all species of Senecio *do. Numbering over 2,000 species in all,* Senecio *can be found in almost every habitat on earth.*

Senecio aquaticus thrives in marshy areas that are wet for most of the year. Most plants die if the soil they grow in is covered with water, because air cannot reach their roots. But marsh-loving plants have many large air spaces inside them to help them survive. Oxygen enters the leaves, which are above water, and travels slowly through the air spaces to the roots.

26

Composites that live high in the mountains are usually short, hugging the ground to avoid the strong winds that sweep along mountainsides. Since the growing season in the mountains is very brief, almost all the species found there are **perennials** (per-EN-ee-uhlz) that live for several years. One growing season in the cool mountains would not be long enough for a plant to sprout from a seed, grow to be an adult, produce flowers, and then make seeds.

27

During its first year, a mountain perennial grows leaves but usually does not produce flowers. It uses its energy to develop a sturdy root system so it can survive long, cold winters. The parts of the plant that are above ground often die back at the end of the growing season. New stems and leaves sprout from the roots the next spring. Since these plants already have roots, they can start growing earlier in the season than plants starting from seed. This allows them to flower and make seeds before the short mountain summer ends.

The blanket flower (Gaillardia) doesn't always produce flowers its first year.

The sea aster (Aster tripolium)

One of the best examples of unusual habitat needs comes from the sea aster, *Aster tripolium.* It grows best in a salty environment that would kill most other land plants. For hundreds of years, the sea aster stayed along the coasts of Britain and northern Europe. Roads were built nearby, but seeds of the sea aster could not survive away from the salty shore.

Then in the winter of 1973, towns along the British coast began spreading rock salt on their roads to combat ice. The salt, dissolved by the melting ice, ran off the roads into the soil nearby. It killed some of the plants growing there but provided a perfect environment for the sea aster. The salt-loving sea aster sprouted along these roads and is now thriving there.

Many composite species around the world are rare and **endangered.** This means that all the members of these species may soon die out. In most cases, they are in danger because their habitat is being changed by humans. For example, when farmers drain marshes to make new fields, marsh-loving species die. When people build houses and roads in areas that had been wild, some species can survive, but the most sensitive species struggle.

One of the world's rarest composites is the desert yellowhead *(Yermo xanthocephalus)*. It lives on only 20 acres (8.1 ha) of land in central Wyoming. The plant's seeds are dispersed by the wind, but they have not been able to take root outside their tiny range. Botanists (plant scientists) don't know why. They think there must be something special about the soil where desert yellowhead grows, but they have not yet discovered what it is.

Rare plants usually get a lot less attention than rare animals, but they are just as important. Plants provide food and shelter for animals and help the soil remain rich in nutrients. Plants are a crucial part of every habitat.

The desert yellowhead (Yermo xanthocephalus) *wasn't discovered until 1990. It is hardy enough to survive the harsh winters and hot summers common in Wyoming.*

Right: *Big sagebrush* (Artemisia tridentata)
Inset: *Many species of sagebrush have small heads clustered on long, thin stalks.*

Sagebrush is not endangered, but it too plays an important role in its habitat. About 20 species of sagebrush live in the western United States, including big sagebrush *(Artemisia tridentata),* which grows up to 10 feet (3.1 m) tall, and black sagebrush *(Artemisia nova),* which rarely grows taller than 1.6 feet (0.5 m). All the sagebrushes are tough plants that can survive the high temperatures and long dry periods common to the Rocky Mountain states.

Wild animals such as the sage grouse and the pygmy rabbit need to have both grass and sagebrush in their habitat. They use grass to hide from predators and as one source of food. Sagebrush provides shelter and nest materials and is a major food source. Its leaves stay rich in protein and fat all year long, and deer, elk, and antelope eat them in late winter when other food is hard to find. These large animals rarely eat sagebrush at other times of the year, because the plant produces several bitter-tasting chemicals and the animals don't like the way it tastes.

32

On one side of the fence, overgrazing has stripped the pasture of all but some spiky sagebrush and yellow-flowered rabbit brush (Chrysothamnus nauseosus). Outside the pasture grows a healthy mix of grasses and other plants.

The addition of livestock ranches to areas where sagebrush lives has drastically changed its habitat. Cattle and sheep don't like the taste of sagebrush either, so they avoid it and eat other plants, such as grasses, instead. When too many of these domestic animals graze in one area for too long, they destroy the tasty plants, leaving sagebrush and other bad-tasting plants behind. Since the mid-1800s, sagebrush has become more common and grasses have almost disappeared in areas that have been heavily grazed. This makes the land less useful for both livestock and wildlife. Some ranchers are now trying to prevent this by not allowing their livestock to graze in one area for too long.

HUMAN USES

Although composites such as sagebrush are not useful to ranchers, many other species have practical uses. In Panama, native people crush the leaves and stems of a plant they call *guaco* (GWAH-koh; *Clibadium sylvestre*), then toss them into a stream. The crushed plant releases a poison that stuns fish. The fish then float to the surface, where the people collect them for food. The poison does not harm people who eat the fish.

Other useful chemicals made by some composites are pyrethrins (py-RETH-rins). Pyrethrins are powerful insecticides. They protect the plants that make them from being eaten by insects. Pyrethrins can be removed from composites to make insecticides that farmers and gardeners can use. Sprayed on plants that don't produce their own pyrethrins, these products ward off many kinds of insect pests. Pyrethrins can also be made in chemical laboratories.

The chrysanthemum *is one composite that makes its own pyrethrins. These chemicals can be removed from the plant to make insecticides.*

Yarrow (Achillea millefolium)

Burdock (Arctium)

Goatsbeard, or yellow salsify (Tragopogon dubius)

Of course, not all composites are capable of causing harm. Folk medicines made from the leaves or roots of composites have been used by people all over the world. Fresh leaves of the yarrow *(Achillea millefolium)*, soaked in water and placed in the nostrils, were used to stop nosebleeds. Tea made with burdock roots was used to relieve skin rashes. Native Americans chewed dried sap from the goatsbeard *(Tragopogon)* to prevent stomach problems. Chemists are beginning to study these old remedies to try to find new drugs.

Cutting a dandelion stem reveals the white sap inside.

Latex from the guayule *bush* (Parthenium argentatum, background) *was used to make the rubber in this tire.*

The milky sap found in many composite species contains latex, a gooey liquid that can be used to make rubber. Sap from *guayule* (gwah-YOO-lay; *Parthenium argentatum*), a Mexican shrub, is added to artificial rubber to make it more flexible. Even dandelions *(Taraxacum officinale)* contain some latex, but it would take millions of plants to make enough rubber for one automobile tire.

A few composites are even useful as food crops. The roots of chicory *(Cichorium intybus)* can be dried and ground into a powder used to brew a coffeelike drink. This was especially common during World War II, when coffee was unavailable or very expensive. Chicory "coffee" is still popular today in the southern United States, either blended with regular coffee or alone. Leaves of lettuce *(Lactuca sativa)* and endive *(Cichorium endivia)* are used in salads.

Right: *Chicory* (Cichorium intybus)
Below: *Red leaf lettuce* (Lactuca sativa)

Another composite with a special use is the Jerusalem artichoke *(Helianthus tuberosus)*. No one knows for sure where its name came from. This plant is not from Jerusalem (it's native to North America), and it is not an artichoke. It is a perennial sunflower that can reach 10 feet tall (3.1 m) and has many heads. The Jerusalem artichoke plant grows thick, knobby roots called tubers. Like a more common tuber, the potato, it can be cooked and eaten. It was one of the first foods explorers of North America took back to Europe.

Jerusalem artichoke tubers are special because they are one of the few plants that contain chemicals called **fructans,** which can be made into a sweet sugar called fructose. People with the disease diabetes can eat little or no table sugar, but fructose does not harm them.

The head of a Jerusalem artichoke (Helianthus tuberosus) *looks a lot like a sunflower head, but its roots look more like potatoes.*

Sunflowers seem to follow the sun, facing eastward at sunrise and turning slowly to face westward by sunset. However, scientists have determined that sunflowers don't do this any more than other flowering plants do. Their name probably comes from their bright sunny color and starlike shape.

The most important crop plant among composites is the common sunflower. Humans have used sunflower seeds as a source of food and oil for thousands of years. At one time, Native Americans collected seeds from wild sunflowers that grew near their villages. Later, they started planting and caring for the sunflowers along with their corn, beans, and other crops.

By saving seeds from some of their sunflower plants, Native Americans developed varieties with features like larger heads and larger seeds. Other varieties were bred for the color or pattern of the achene's shell. Some shells were all black, some were all white, and some were striped. One variety had achenes with purple shells. The Hopi people boiled these shells to make a purple dye they used to color baskets.

Native Americans were the first to eat sunflower seeds—either raw or roasted, much as people do now. They roasted seeds and ground them into flour for bread, or they pounded them to release an oil for cooking and making body paint.

Mature heads of the Mammoth Russian sunflower

In the late 1500s, European settlers saw how Native Americans used sunflowers and sent some seeds back to their home countries. Now sunflowers are grown in many areas of Europe and Asia too. Russian farmers, in particular, have developed many new varieties and new methods for cultivating the plant. One of their prize creations is the Mammoth Russian, which grows over 12 feet (3.7 meters) high and has a head that measures 2 feet (0.6 meters) across.

Modern farmers have continued to breed varieties of sunflowers with different features. Some have seeds richer in protein, and others have seeds richer in fat. Protein-rich sunflower seeds are good eating—for both humans and birds. Fat-rich seeds are used to make sunflower oil. This oil contains a lot of linoleic (lin-uh-LAY-ick) acid, which is important for the health of human nerve cells. These are the cells in our brain and spinal cord that control how our bodies function. Oils made from other plants, such as corn, don't contain much linoleic acid. Scientists are now testing whether eating sunflower oil might help people who have diseases of the nervous system, such as multiple sclerosis.

Sunflowers can be used in other ways too. The oil is an ingredient of linoleum and some kinds of paint. The stalks can be dried and burned like firewood, split to make narrow shingles, or chopped up and fed to livestock.

Gardeners have bred special kinds of sunflowers with larger heads, bigger rays, or unusual colors, like these dark red ones.

Ragweed (Ambrosia trifida)

The sunflower family includes many beautiful plants such as daisies, marigolds, and chrysanthemums that are commonly planted in gardens. But other composite species that spring up in gardens and in farm fields are not welcome there. They are considered **weeds.**

One definition of a weed is that it is any plant growing in a place where people don't want it to grow. But being a weed means more than that. Weeds grow, reproduce, and disperse very quickly. They may produce as many as a million seeds per plant and are usually **annuals** (AN-yoo-uhlz). This means they become full grown and produce seeds within one year. At the end of the growing season, the plants die, but their seeds sprout into new plants the following spring. Some weeds, such as dandelions, grow and reproduce so fast that several generations can develop during a single growing season.

One of the most irritating composite weeds is ragweed. Millions of people who are allergic to its pollen suffer from stuffy noses, weepy eyes, and sneezing fits during the summer, when ragweed pollen is in the air.

A dandelion (above) reproduces so easily, it will make seeds even if its anthers and stigmas arc removed prior to pollination.

The yellow star thistle (Centaurea solstitialis), a weed common in the western United States, is poisonous to livestock.

43

All of these species illustrate how varied and successful the composite family is. Almost anywhere you look—in a garden, by the side of the road, or in the wild—you will find composites. All have heads of many small florets crowded together. All make hard-shelled achenes to carry their seeds. Beyond this, composites differ from each other in many ways. They come in all sizes and colors, and have developed ways to live in dozens of different habitats. The familiar sunflower, with its tall stalk and bright yellow head, is just one member of this large and diverse family.

GLOSSARY

achene: a structure that contains a seed and has a hard outer shell

adapt: to change in order to survive in an environment

annual: a plant that sprouts from a seed, flowers, produces new seeds, and dies within one year or growing season

anther: the puffy tip of a stamen that contains tiny grains carrying sperm

bract: a tough, leaflike structure on the back of a composite head

bur: a prickly structure containing one or more seeds or seed containers (achenes). Burs stick easily to clothing or animal fur to help the seeds spread to new places.

cross-fertilization: the process in which a sperm unites with an egg from a different plant

disk: the circle at the center of a composite head in which many small flowers are crowded together

disperse: to cause seeds to be spread some distance from the parent plant

endangered: at risk of losing all members of a species forever

fertilize: to unite a sperm with an egg to create a seed

floret: one of the small flowers that make up a composite head. Disk florets are located in the center of the head, and ray florets are located along the rim.

fructans: natural sugars produced by Jerusalem artichokes that can be eaten safely by people with diabetes

habitat: the kind of environment in which a species normally lives. A habitat includes the type of soil, amount of rain and sunshine, range of temperature, and kinds of animals and plants that live there.

head: a cluster of many small flowers that looks like one large flower

involucre: the structure that forms the back of a composite head and holds together the many small flowers that make up the head. In some species, the involucre also helps a plant spread its seeds to new places.

nectar: a sweet liquid held in pockets at the base of the petals of a flower and drunk by insects

ovary: an egg chamber located at the base of the style

pappus: a ring of hairs, bristles, or scales on the top of some kinds of seed containers (achenes). Like a sail, a large pappus allows the wind to carry the seed away from the parent plant.

perennial: a plant that lives for several years, and that may not flower until it is two or more years old

pollen: tiny grains produced by the male parts of flowers. Each grain contains two sperm.

pollinate: to bring pollen into contact with the sticky stigmas of a composite flower

self-fertilization: the process by which an egg joins with a sperm from the same plant

stamen: one of five long, thin male structures that surround the style and produce sperm

stigmas: two arms that form when the tip of the style splits. Their sticky inner surfaces collect tiny grains containing sperm to join with the egg.

style: the female structure in the center of a composite flower. The egg is housed in a chamber at its base.

taproot: a single large root with which some plants reach water deep in the earth

weed: a plant that grows and reproduces quickly, and is found in areas where humans are trying to grow other plants

INDEX

ABOUT THE AUTHOR

Author **Cherie Winner** is a wildflower watcher in the way some people are bird-watchers and enjoys hiking near her home in Wyoming. Recently she trekked over hot sagebrush plains in search of the rare desert yellowhead. As usual, she had her camera along and captured it on film (see page 31). In researching *The Sunflower Family*, Dr. Winner also discovered a new pastime: hanging out in the Rocky Mountain Herbarium, learning about plants and the scientists who study them. Dr. Winner is the author of two other Carolrhoda Nature Watch titles, *Coyotes* and *Salamanders*.

ABOUT THE PHOTOGRAPHER

Sherry Shahan is a writer and photographer whose assignments have taken her on horseback with gauchos in Argentina, riding with a musher in the Iditarod dogsled race in Alaska, and climbing Ayers Rock in Australia. And those are just the *A*'s! Ms. Shahan lives in Templeton, California.